14 Ways To Market Your Book Like A Bestselling Author

Written By

Dante Fortson

14 Ways To Market Your Book Like A Bestselling Author
Copyright © 2014 by Dante Fortson

Website: www.virtualbusinesstrainingnetwork.com

ISBN 10: 1495433307
ISBN 13: 978-1495433306

All rights reserved. No portion of this book may be reproduced or transmitted in any form or by any means, electronic or mechanical, including photocopying, recording, or by an information storage and retrieval system, without the written permission of the author.

First Edition. Printed in the United States of America

Published by: Impact Agenda Media

Table of Contents

Introduction: An Accidental Bestselling Author

- The Failure of My First Book
- From Unknown To Bestseller In 70 Days
- My Life As A Professional Writer

Chapter 1: I'm Creating A Marketing Monster

1. What Is Neuro Linguistic Programming?
2. Act Like A Fan, Think Like A Stalker
3. You Don't Know What You Don't Know

Chapter 2: Writing The Book Was The Easy Part

4. 10 Reasons You Need To Be Blogging
5. Bribe Your Way To A Fan Base
6. No Author Is An Island
7. Tapping Your Inner Influence

Chapter 3: Your Schedule Is Killing Your Book Sales

8. A Bronx Tale Marketing Lesson

9. The 80/20 Rule of Marketing
10. Put Your Best Pen Forward
11. Bending Social Media To Your Will

Chapter 4: Any Niche Is Yours For The Taking

12. Just Take The Credibility You Want
13. The Omnipresent Author
14. Bestsellers Do It Better

Appendix A: Marketing Checklist
Appendix B: Marketing Resources

Introduction

I bet you're wondering why I didn't indent this paragraph, aren't you? The real question is, would you have noticed it if I hadn't pointed it out? I'm going to let you in on a little secret, but not right now.

This book isn't going to teach you any "magic formulas" and I can't guarantee you any specific financial results, but it will show you proven marketing techniques that I've learned little by little since 1999. I hope my constant use of contractions isn't bothering you, but if they are, I'll come back to that soon as well.

The Failure of My First Book

When I wrote my first book, Religion and Relationship, I knew very little about actual marketing. Most of what I knew was based on gimmicks that I'd seen work in Internet Marketing, but they weren't nearly as effective in my niche, which at the time was Christian Inspiration. That kicked off my journey to unlearn all of my bad marketing habits.

Religion and Relationship partly consisted of my personal story and partly of lessons I've learned from

Introduction

the Bible. It's still one of my favorite books that I've written, but I had no clue how to market it effectively.

I was very optimistic after I sold ten copies at my very small church book signing, but I soon found out that selling books wasn't as easy as I thought it would be. No matter what I did, I just couldn't get people interested, and I couldn't figure out why.

Over the first year, I sold maybe ten copies total, after the book signing. That number was spirit crushing. In fact, it took so long to sell those ten, that I hadn't even checked my royalty account until I got ready to publish my soon to be bestselling book, As The Days of Noah Were. I'll come back to As The Days of Noah Were in a few minutes.

There were several reasons for the failure of Religion and Relationship. However, there was one big reason that I didn't quit, but I'll come back to that.

Introduction

1. Religion and Relationship's failure wasn't because it was poorly written, but because it was poorly marketed.
2. In addition to my terrible marketing efforts, I had no clue how to build a fan base of loyal readers.

I thought I was doing everything right. I had a few writers that posted reviews of the book online, and I even started my own ministry blog. So here's what went wrong.

My blog started off getting about 40 visitors per day consistently after about a week or so into writing, but I didn't have a mailing list set up to capture the emails of interested readers. Because of that, I lost the opportunity to reconnect with them at a later date and possibly sell them a book.

This is when I started to really dig into marketing and promoting my book, but I was honestly ready to quit writing and get a job. Thankfully, I did land a job at a local Christian newspaper, which paid me to write. The owner of the paper had read Religion and

Introduction

Relationship, loved it, and hired me at the interview.

During my time at the paper, I managed to get a good review from the lady that wrote book reviews. I'd actually sent it to her before I started writing for them, which is how the owner managed to read it in the first place. From there, I met Brenda Ward, host of Open Book Radio at KKVV (the local Christian station). I booked an interview with her and managed to sell a few more books.

During my brief stint at the paper, I absorbed as much as I could learn about the publishing business, marketing, and writing. I was also working on my second book as well. That's when a friend of mine and I stumbled upon a genius idea.

From Unknown To Bestseller In 70 Days

My second book was based around a subject that I'd been interested in and taking notes on since I was in high school. At some point, I decided to compile them into a book, but I was still a little discouraged

Introduction

and hesitant from the lack of sales of Religion and Relationship.

One afternoon, while talking on the phone with my friend, we started discussing Coast To Coast and thought it would be cool to have our own radio show. I knew a little bit about podcasting from way back in the day when I use to interview local underground rappers. We decided on the name, The Omega Hour, and our goal was to interview authors and discuss the supernatural from a Biblical perspective. So, I set up an account for the show and contacted our first potential guest.

After our first interview, I dropped that guests' name to book my second guest, who is a bestselling Christian author. After that, I just rinsed and repeated for two years, building a huge list of well known and unknown Christian authors, speakers, and TV hosts.

All during our first year, we talked about my coming book, As The Days of Noah Were, and people were seriously interested. In fact, I started receiving emails almost every week asking me for a release date.

By this time, I had a mailing list set up, and the success of the podcast was growing my website readership. My website was now averaging just over 100 people per day and my mailing list was at just over 300 people.

Becoming a bestseller in just 70 days after releasing my book independently wasn't by design. In fact, I had no clue that by us talking about the book, we were pre-marketing it and building a buzz. That 70 day success was 365 days in the making.

As The Days of Noah Were was published August 18, 2010 and it hit the Amazon Bestseller list on Kindle™ October 27, 2010. That's exactly 70 days after its release. When I checked my rank that morning, I was in the top five in three categories:

- #1: Old Testament Study
- #5: New Testament Study
- #5: Prophecies

Introduction

Over the next year, my sales stayed consistent as we continued the show, and continued talking about the book. It is now 2014 and As The Days of Noah Were has been on the Amazon Top 100 Bestsellers list in those categories since 2010.

That is not an easy status to maintain in a field that has thousands of books to choose from, some written by mega televangelists that you've probably seen on TV. As we continue through this book, I'm going to share some of those strategies with you, so that you can do it for yourself.

The first bit of advice I want to give you right here in the introduction is to build buzz around your book. Talk about it before its done and let people know what it's all about.

My Life As A Professional Writer

Writing a bestselling book has opened a lot of doors for me. At one point, Open Book Radio booked me for an entire month to discuss the book in depth. Af-

Introduction

ter my final show, the owner of the radio station called and asked for me before I left. He told me that my series of shows were the most responded to shows in the history of the radio station.

It was my experience as an internet radio host that gave me the experience I needed to connect with the audience, speak in short sentences, and direct the host in the direction that I wanted to take the interview. There is an art to being on the radio, being likeable, and being memorable.

My second bit of advice to you as an author is to learn "radio speak". Know when to end your sentences, let the host jump in to keep the flow going, don't talk for long periods of time, and end in a way that guides the host in the direction that you want the interview to go.

Over the years, I've done over 100 hours of interviews as either the interviewer or interviewee. I've been on Christian and non Christian radio shows. I've debated and I've filled in as a spontaneous guest

Introduction

host several times. Having that experience is priceless.

The great part about focusing most of my efforts on internet radio is that people still find those shows on the internet and contact me on my website. Partially because of that and my newly learned marketing efforts, my total number of subscribers has grown from 300 to over 17,000 at the time of this writing.

Since the success of As The Days of Noah Were, I've written and published several other books, one of which (Beyond Flesh and Blood) hit the Amazon Bestsellers list as well, but not as high on the list. I now make a steady income from blogging and marketing my books online, along with several other opportunities that have come about over the years.

There are quite a few things that I've learned since releasing Religion and Relationship in 2009, and I'm going to share a few of those with you before we get into the meat of this book.

Introduction

1. If people can connect with what you're saying, they want to hear more of what you have to say. Be relatable.

2. Throw the rules out the window and do what works for you. Be a rebel.

Let's pause at #2 for a moment. In the beginning of this introduction, I pointed out that there were no indents and that I was using a lot of contractions. There are two very good reasons for me to point that out:

1. I'm writing this how I talk. It's called conversational tone, and most people don't talk "proper" when conversing with people. There are exceptions to this, and one of them is when you're writing something that calls for a scholarly and professional tone.

2. I didn't indent because we live in the age of blogging, and very few bloggers indent. People are getting used to reading blogs, so a

Introduction

book that reads like a blog connects on a subconscious social level.

I'm going to end this introduction by saying that the world of marketing is only limited by your imagination and ambition. By learning the basic principles and building on them, you too can learn to market your book like a bestselling author.

Enjoy,

Dante Fortson

"Failure doesn't mean you are a failure it just means you haven't succeeded yet." – Robert H. Schuller

Chapter 1: I'm Creating A Marketing Monster

That's right. By the time you finish this chapter, you'll be light years ahead of most people in your niche. Here's what you're going to learn:

- The basics of Neuro Linguistic Programming.
- How to get information from your readers.
- What you don't know about marketing.

This single chapter has the potential to completely change the way you've been doing almost everything in your marketing efforts so far.

Before you continue, if you skipped the Introduction, go back and read it because I'll be making references to it throughout the book. If you have already read it, let's get started.

What Is Neuro Linguistic Programming?

This is a concept that we are all familiar with, but very few of us know what it's called. Also known as NLP, Neuro Linguistic Programming is a very technical way of saying; you can change people's behavior by changing the words you use. Isn't that an awesome concept?

Now I'm going to completely change your paradigm, if you've never realized how this works. I can guarantee that you've been on the receiving end of NLP before. Let's start with a very simple exercise. I'm going to say same exact thing three different ways and I want you to consider how each one makes you feel. It's important that you actually pause and consider your emotional response, so make sure you do it.

1. Get my drink and you better hurry up!
2. I need a drink. Got get it for me.
3. I'm a little thirsty. Would you please get me a drink? Thank you.

How did each of those statements make you feel? Which one of those statements is most likely to get a positive response from you? How you say things is a lot more important than what you're saying.

Chapter 1: I'm Creating A Marketing Monster

Now I'm going to give you three more sentences, and again, I want you to think about how they make you feel.

This time, I want to give you a common scenario. You've just screwed up on your job and your boss has just found out, so he sends you an email:
1. You idiot! Get back over there and do it again!
2. Get back over there now and fix it or you're fired!
3. You're doing a great job, but you made a little mistake. I'd appreciate it, if you would go back and fix it for me. Thank you.

Again, how did those sentences make you feel? Which one is most likely to get a good response from you? Which one is most likely to make you want to punch your boss in the face?

In both examples, the three sentences all had the same goals in mind. In one example, the person wanted a drink. In the second example, the boss needed you to fix a mistake.

If you're not into being verbally abused, chances are that in both examples, sentence #3 was most likely to get the desired response from you. There is a reason for that.

In the first example, the person connected with you by saying they were thirsty. We've all experienced thirst before and it's not a great feeling. They then followed their statement with a question that gives you the option of saying no. Finally, they thanked you as if you had already completed the task. Subconsciously, you feel the need to earn that "thank you" that was already given.

In the second example, the boss starts off by complimenting you and acknowledging your efforts, thus fulfilling your subconscious need for recognition. He then followed it by calling your mistake "little", which removes some of the pressure and apprehension of receiving a reprimand from an authority figure. Next, he let you know that your extra effort will be appreciated, which shows that your effort is not being taken for granted. Finally, they thank you as if

Chapter 1: I'm Creating A Marketing Monster

you had already completed the task, which goes back to the subconscious need to earn the thank you.

Certain words and phrases have a drastically better chance of getting the results that you desire. Saying "please" and "thank you" usually works best in almost every case. People love to feel appreciated and that what they are doing is making a difference.

You can also use this strategy when contacting important people within your niche or their assistants. This isn't anything new. Most parents teach their children the basic concept of saying please and thank you, and those same lessons can be applied to the world of business.

The key here is not to over abuse this power in everyday life. What you want to do is consider how you word your marketing materials. Consider how it makes the reader feel, and cater to their subconscious desires. Here are some questions to consider when designing your marketing material, blogging, or emailing clients and fans.

- Does your sales pitch sound like you're only concerned with getting their hard earned money, or does it sound like you want to make a valuable contribution to their lives?
- When you respond to questions and comments, does your response show appreciate and concern, or obligation and disdain?

These are things that you need to keep in mind as you write and speak. Yes, speaking is important too. Practice changing how you speak to people, and you will see better results. If you have a fear of public speaking, contact Toastmaster International to sign up for public speaking and leadership classes (Appendix B).

What I've shown you is just the tip of the iceberg when it comes to NLP, but if you practice these basic concepts, not only will you experience positive changes in your marketing efforts, you will also experience positive changes in your everyday life.

Chapter 1: I'm Creating A Marketing Monster

Act Like A Fan, Think Like A Stalker

The best marketers know almost everything there is to know about their fans, just like stalkers know everything about the person they are stalking. The technical term is "demographics", which usually includes the following:

- Age
- Ethnicity
- Gender
- City
- State
- Country
- Income
- Education

All of these factors tie into how different marketing material is produced. By knowing just a few of these, you can create a sales strategy that is more likely to attract a buyer in your desired target market.

I haven't met you in person, most likely, but I can tell you quite a few things about yourself that you probably don't know that I know. And now, I'm going to read your mind.

1. You've either written a book or information product or you're thinking about doing it.
2. You're at a point in your passion for writing where you either want to make money or you want to make more money.
3. You would love to quit your job and make a living as a professional writer, but you don't sell enough books to do so.
4. You put way too much pressure on yourself to be the best writer that you can be because you think it will lead to great opportunities.
5. You can't understand why people aren't buying your book, even though it's really good.

How did I do? It's not by chance that I know the above. Those are all of the factors that went into the creation of the title of this book. Before I started writing, I sat down and figured out exactly who I wanted to reach. In other words, my target market.

Chapter 1: I'm Creating A Marketing Monster

If most of the above describes you, I'm going to let you in on a little secret: being a successful writer and being a "good" writer are two vastly different things. An OK writer can be very successful while a good writer can be very unsuccessful.

When it comes to writing, the definition of "good" is as relative as it gets. A good writer knows what their readers want to read. A good writer knows how to get their point across without a lot of extra fluff to pad the page count. That happens by knowing more about your reader than they know about themselves. You accomplish this by going beyond the usual demographic data. Here are some examples from my personal journey as a writer.

When I first got started, I was adamant about getting my book printed in hardcover, but a poll on my website revealed that:

- 51.35% prefer paperback books.
- 27.03% prefer ebooks (PDF or Kindle).
- 21.62% prefer hardcover, but will still read paperback or ebooks.

Based on the results of the poll, I stopped wasting my time pursuing a hardcover option, when over 76% of my readers didn't want it, and the few that did were fine with the options that I was already offering.

I'm going to give you one more example of gathering information about your readers. Recently, I started developing a free online course that teaches people how to start their own online ministry.

While only 8.06% of my readers enjoyed "How To" books, another poll showed that 46.77% wanted to run their own website and 33.87% want to run their own online ministry.

What that means for me is that there is a smaller niche, within the niche that I'm currently in. I have over 100 polls on my website, each specifically designed to collect data relevant to what I do. If you already have a website or blog, you should be collecting data as well. I'm going to come back to why you should have a blog in Chapter 2, but if you al-

Chapter 1: I'm Creating A Marketing Monster

ready have one, you need to install the Wordpress plugin "wp-polls" (Appendix B).

The secret is to drop a poll in your articles every once in a while. Make sure you have an end goal in mind for the data that you collect. In the end, it will help you take your future projects to the next level.

You Don't Know What You Don't Know

I'm going to fill you in on ten of the big mistakes that I've made over the last five years. The reason I'm doing this is so that you can fix them if you're making the same mistakes, or avoid them if you haven't made them yet.

The best way to use this section to your advantage is to Google the problems that I faced and compare the solutions that you find, to the solutions that I came up with through trial and error.

1. The very first mistake I made when writing Religion and Relationship was not talking about it until it was finished. When I wrote,

As The Days of Noah Were, I talked about it for almost a year before its release in 2010, and I'm still talking about it now in 2014.

2. The next mistake I made was thinking that people cared that I wrote Religion and Relationship. The truth is that nobody cares unless you make them care. Don't be afraid to tell them why they should care about your book.

3. Book signings are less productive than book fairs. When I was trying to get the word out about Religion and Relationship, I tried setting up book signings, and missed out on several book fairs, which almost always have a much higher turnout, unless you're famous already.

4. Internet radio can be just as effective as traditional radio. Traditional radio may reach 100,000 listeners at one time (example). Internet radio has the potential to reach millions over the course of time. Unless your interview gets replayed on the radio (not likely), once it's done, anyone that missed it is

Chapter 1: I'm Creating A Marketing Monster

out of luck. With internet radio, it's available 24/7.

5. I mentioned it in the Introduction, but I didn't collect email addresses when I first started. That means I had no way of keeping in touch with people that had bought my book or with people that might want to buy my book in the future. Start building your mailing list from the beginning.

6. For the first two years, I focused a majority of my time on blogging as much as I could, thinking that it would help increase book sales. I was dead wrong. Ultimately, it was my radio show that made the biggest difference starting out. While blogging can increase sales, you'll have to check out Chapter 3 to find out why you don't need to spend so much time doing it.

7. Perhaps one of the most time consuming things that I did as an independent author was trying to get distribution in local stores. I had

the option of paying a $40.00 fee to have Amazon do it for me, but I was too dumb to take advantage of it. When I released As The Days of Noah Were, the price had gone down to $25.00, so I signed up. Now my books are sold at Barnes and Noble, hundreds of online book retailers, small mom and pop book stores across the nation, and even a few local bookstores that turned me down originally. Take advantage of anything that Amazon is offering you at a ridiculously cheap price.

8. After As The Days of Noah Were became an Amazon bestseller, I stopped trying to promote Religion and Relationship. In reality, this was the perfect time to promote it. Don't stop promoting your older work just because you have something new out. Sometimes it takes years for something to catch on and start selling. Marketing is a marathon after the sprint is over.

9. When I first started writing, I wrote how I thought how I was supposed to write, because

Chapter 1: I'm Creating A Marketing Monster

I hadn't found my own voice and style yet. What you are reading now is my voice, my style, and my rules. Following the rules of writing won't make you a great writer; it makes you an obedient writer that doesn't stand out from the crowd. Find your voice and stand out.

10. Finally, I took the advice of another author that was afraid to be controversial because it might alienate his fan base. Screw that. Be controversial if it's something you believe in. Some people will love it, some people will hate it, but everyone will talk about you because they have an opinion on it. Don't try to please everyone all of the time. The people that matter don't mind and the people that mind don't matter.

Hopefully you take my advice and start assessing your own situation. The more of these mistakes that you can avoid the better off you'll be. Most important of all, you need to find your own voice as quickly as possible.

"In order to succeed, your desire for success should be greater than your fear of failure." – Bill Cosby

Chapter 2: Writing The Book Was The Easy Part

That's right, writing the book was the easy part. If you thought it was difficult and time consuming, you're in for a huge reality check. It's the bumpy road after your book is released that most authors get lost on.

Now that your book is complete, it's time to start the long road to establishing yourself as an expert in your field. The best way to start doing that is by creating a blog. My personal recommendation is Wordpress (Appendix B).

10 Reasons You Need To Be Blogging

When I speak of blogging, I'm not talking about setting up a free blog on Wordpress.com. I'm talking about paying for your own website hosting and domain name on your own website.

1. Having your own website and domain name shows people that you are serious about what you do. Anyone can set up a free blog any time they want, but websites cost money.

Most people won't waste their time investing in something that they aren't serious about.

2. Blogging gives you a chance to have your voice heard beyond the words in your book. If you feel like you have more to contribute to your subject than your book can cover, blogging is a good way to reach your audience. With your blog, you can write about various subjects, news stories, major events, or new findings related to your book, and link to your book within the article. This is a great way to increase sales.

3. Having a blog gives you the opportunity to build a list of repeat readers by collecting their email addresses. As people have more positive experiences with you, their loyalty grows, which in the long term means more book sales. The numbers vary, depending on the source, but it usually takes 5-7 positive interactions with a person before someone will make a purchase.

Chapter 2: Writing The Book Was The Easy Part

4. Having your own blog allows more people to find you via search engines. As you write about topics related to your book, search engines pick up your articles and bring people to your website. This allows you to reach people that you probably wouldn't have been able to otherwise. The more specific your topics of choice, the better your chances of gaining readers that want to buy what you have to offer.

5. When you are ready to expand your niche, having a blog lets you do that simply by publishing a series of articles on your website. This is something that you want to do slowly because you don't want to neglect your loyal fan base. If you want to break into a new niche that compliments your current niche, do it slowly by writing an article once a month and ease into it over time.

6. If you ever decide to write more books, make an audio or video product, you don't have to start from scratch. You can use your blog to

tell your readers about your new project. If you have been consistently growing your email list, you can expect more sales faster when you release new material.

7. Having your own blog gives you the opportunity to make more income, not necessarily directly related to writing or blogging. Some of those opportunities include, but are not limited to:

   a. Advertising
   b. Affiliate Sales
   c. Donations
   d. Consulting
   e. Monthly Memberships

8. Having your own blog gives you the opportunity to connect with other authors and bloggers in your niche. Networking can be a great way to expand your fan base and increase sales as well. Other authors and bloggers take you seriously when you have your own website instead of a free one. It also shows that you can

Chapter 2: Writing The Book Was The Easy Part

help them gain exposure in front of your audience as well. A free Wordpress blog is not enough, and a Facebook fan page is not enough.

9. Having your own blog gives your fans the opportunity to share your content all over the internet. Social sharing can be one of the fastest ways to expand your fan base and increase you rankings in the search engines. Digg Digg is a great social sharing plugin for Wordpress (Appendix B)

10. Finally, having your own blog gives you the opportunity to market your own products, repeatedly, to a captive audience that already has an interest in what you do. This goes back to what I mentioned about needing 5-7 positive experiences with a person before they make a purchase.

These are just ten of the reasons that you should have your own blog. Depending on your niche, you may be able to think of more, but if you're struggling to make book sales and you don't have a blog, you need to get one now not later. If you do have a blog and you're still struggling, find your voice and read Chapter 3.

Bribe Your Way To A Fan Base

I've been doing a lot of talking about having subscribers and building a mailing list. Now I'm going to show you the strategies that I've used to build my list to over 18,000 subscribers at the time of this writing.

The first thing you have to decide is whether or not you want to pay to maintain your list. Feedburner is the option that I use. It's free and it's owned by Google, so it's likely not going anywhere any time soon.

Aweber (Appendix B) is a paid service that is used by tens of thousands of people. The downside is that, as more people subscriber, the more you have to pay for the service. The upside is that you get tons of

Chapter 2: Writing The Book Was The Easy Part

detailed statistics that are useful in helping you market your book.

Feel free to Google and compare the two, because once you decide, the list building strategy works the same either way.

There are basically three prime locations to place a subscription box on your website.

1. At the top of the sidebar.
2. At the center of your content.
3. At the bottom of your content.

If you have these three locations covered, feel free to experiment with putting the box anywhere else on your site to see what gives you the best results.

After you have your subscription boxes set up, you'll want to offer visitors something of value that interests them. This can be a free report that you right specifically for this purpose, a free audio, or free video. If people feel that it will provide value to them, they will give you their email address in exchange for the information.

Another good strategy is to talk about upcoming articles or other projects, and let them know that they should subscribe so that they don't miss out. Nobody wants to miss out on something that might be useful to them.

If you take the time to consistently implement these strategies, they will pay off big time in the end.

No Author Is An Island

An island, by definition, stands alone, surrounded lots of water. There's really no deeper hidden meaning there, so don't waste your time looking for one. My point is, you're not an island, and you don't have to stand alone.

Your fans are more than willing to join in and help you with your marketing efforts, but you have to be willing to tell them what you need and why you need

Chapter 2: Writing The Book Was The Easy Part

it. Here are a few ideas for getting fans to share your work:

1. At the end of you book, thank them for reading it and ask them to share it with everyone they know.

2. At the end of every blog post, ask your readers to share your content on Facebook, Twitter, Linked In, etc.

Another great way to get the word out is by giving away bookmarks, business cards, and excerpts from your book. Even if someone doesn't buy your book immediately, your bookmark becomes a constant "in your face" reminder every time they use it to read another book.

By adding a QR code to your free material, anyone that comes in contact with it can scan it and buy your book, or check out your website. It's completely up to you how you choose to set up your QR codes.

That brings me to the next strategy that very few authors are doing on a big scale. You can turn every book you sell into a massive marketing machine all its own.

QR Codes have completely changed the way we separate digital from physical products. In the 2nd edition of my book, As The Days of Noah Were, I used QR codes to facilitate discussion after every chapter. In addition to that, I used them to add over 20 hours worth of audio and video, spread throughout each chapter.

If done right, QR codes can be that "wow factor" that makes your book worth sharing. You can get QR codes for free online (Appendix B).

The final point I want to make in this section is that you need to reach out to other authors and bloggers in the same niche. If you're expanding, you need to reach out to authors and bloggers in other niches.

This kind of collaboration is often referred to as a joint venture (JV) or guest blogging, depending on

Chapter 2: Writing The Book Was The Easy Part

the arrangement. Just so you understand the difference, I'm going to break down both of them for you.

1. Joint Ventures (JV) is usually an arrangement between two or more people, in which they all agree to promote the project of one person, in exchange for a commission. An example of this would be getting five bloggers to tell their followers about your latest book release. In return, they would receive a percentage of each sale that they refer to you.

2. Guest blogging is when another blogger allows you to write content for their audience, and you receive credit for the article, along with a link back to your website, or vise versa. This can be very effective in giving you exposure to an entirely new audience.

I know you're probably wondering how you go about setting up a joint venture, and I'm going to help you out. There are two options that I have personally used, so those are the only two that I'm going to suggest.

1. Clickbank.com is one of, if not the biggest site for affiliate products. The positive is that there are tons of people out there that will jump at the chance to promote your product for you. The downside is the amount of time it takes to setup the required pages, the generous 50% or more commission that comes out of your profit, and the $50.00 setup fee.

2. Amazon Associates is one of the oldest affiliate programs around. Unlike Clickbank, there are no additional pages required to get started and no setup fees. The downside is that the commission ranges from 4% - 8.5%, so there are fewer people jumping at the opportunity to promote your books.

Technically, these are more or less considered to be affiliate programs, so absolutely anybody can promote your stuff. However, if you have never done a joint venture before, they are a good place to start.

Ultimately, you have to decide which one you think is right for your joint venture.

Tapping Your Inner Influence

You may not realize it, but you have tons of influence when you take the position of content creator. Content includes books, videos, music, cartoons, blog posts, etc. Whether you believe it or not, you're actually in a very influential position once you start gaining fans.

As I mentioned in the previous section, fans will share your work if you simply ask them to do so, but that's not the extent of your influence. Here are a few examples of other ways you can use your influence within your niche:

- Recommendations are a great example of influencing people. If you've seen a good movie or read a good book, a positive review or comment about it has the power to influence your fans to make a purchase. Siskel and Ebert had a major influence on movies, and because of that, there were many film companies that wanted to pay them for positive reviews, which to my knowledge, they always turned down.

- Political positions are often influenced by people that are on TV. Judge Napolitano used Fox News to influence lots of people to support Ron Paul in the 2012 election primaries, even though everyone else on Fox News was supporting Mitt Romney. He was fired and his show was canceled shortly thereafter, but his fans remained loyal and followed him on his website.

- Charitable causes are a great thing to bring attention to. That is one reason that charities often team up with celebrities. Your influence could help a charity meet a seasonal goal or it could just bring awareness to a much needed organization.

Chapter 2: Writing The Book Was The Easy Part

How you choose to use your new found influence is up to you. Just remember, "With great power comes great responsibility". Use your influence wisely.

"I've failed over and over and over again in my life and that is why I succeed." – Michael Jordan

Chapter 3: Your Schedule Is Killing Your Book Sales

You're probably thinking, "But you don't even know my schedule." You're absolutely right, but I'm willing to bet that your schedule isn't laid out like what I'm about to show you. I'm also willing to bet that your schedule is a lot less focused on marketing than it should be.

A Bronx Tale Marketing Lesson

It's mid day at a quiet bar in the Bronx, when the thunderous sound of Harley Davidson motorcycles break the silence. The bearded and burley biker gang parks their bikes on the curb and enters the bar.

An Italian gentleman in a suit greets them and asks them to leave after they enter because they are not properly dressed. Almost immediately, Sonny enters the bar to see what's going on. The leader of the biker gang says that they only want to have a drink and aren't looking for trouble. Sonny agrees to let them stay.

The bartender politely serves them all a beer, which they shake up and spray all over him. The now angry Sonny walks back into the bar and says, "That wasn't very nice, and now yous gotta leave." The biker replies with, "I'll tell you when the f*** we leave. Get the f*** outta here."

Sonny doesn't say a word. He quietly walks over to the door, locks it, turns around and says, "Now yous can't leave."

Whenever someone visits your website for the first time, your content should say, "Now yous can't leave." YouTube is the perfect example of this strategy.

How many times have you gone to YouTube to watch one video and before you know it, you're ten videos in and completely off track? That's exactly what my personal website does (www.MinisterFortson.com). I'm going to share a few numbers with you and then I'm going to tell you how you can do the same thing with your website.

Chapter 3: Your Schedule Is Killing Your Book Sales

1. Bounce Rate - This is a calculation of the percentage of people that look at one page on your site and leave immediately after. The bounce rate on my site is 19.30%. That means 80.70% of the people that come to my site check out more than one page before leaving.

2. Average Page Views - This is a calculation of the average number of pages that each visitor looks at before leaving your website. The average number of page views per visitor on my site is 18.

3. Average Time On Site - This is a calculation of the average amount of time someone spends on your website before leaving. The average time spent on my site is 38 minutes 05 seconds.

In case you're wondering, those numbers are well above average. Feel free to compare my stats to any other site on the web at www.alexa.com.

My site wasn't always like that, but when I started rebranding and repositioning myself, I decided to copy YouTube and Amazon. I firmly believe that if you're going to mimic something, you mimic the best.

The following list details the changes that I made to my site during the makeover. Hopefully, some of these suggestions will help you optimize your site so that people stay longer and subscribe more often.

1. The very first thing I did was choose a new template that was more flexible than my old template. The difficult part was finding a theme that kept my color scheme (red, black, white), while allowing me to make the major changes that I had in mind.

2. After I'd installed my new them, I was pretty satisfied with the new look. A short time later, I ended up on a website of an author that had a different sidebar on his book sales page than he did on his home page. It was the first time I'd seen it done on a Wordpress blog, so I

Chapter 3: Your Schedule Is Killing Your Book Sales

found the plugin that allowed me to do it as well. For more information on the Custom Sidebars plugin see Appendix B.

3. The next thing I did was start a forum, but it didn't catch on. After about a month, I got rid of it. However, just because my forum didn't catch on doesn't mean it won't if you add one to your site. Forums are a good way to keep people coming back and to add a social element based around your website.

4. The chat window was next, but I ended up getting rid of that too. People used it, but not consistently enough to justify keeping it. Again, that shouldn't stop you from adding one to your site if you want.

5. One day I had the bright idea to add a scrolling news marquee to the top of the site. People loved it, so I kept it for a long time until I replaced it with the content slider that is currently on the site.

6. The next major change involved my sidebar again. I experimented with a couple of different options but settled on a sidebar that let me add custom pictures to it, along with a description (Appendix B). From there I fiddled around with the CSS and changed the link color so that it stood out more.

7. The next step was to add pictures next to the excerpts on my home page to draw people's attention to other articles. This required the Thumbnail For Excerpts plugin (Appendix B)

8. The last change I'd made, at the time of this writing, is the part that was inspired by YouTube and Amazon. Both Amazon and YouTube show you similar items or videos no matter what page you land on while on their sites, so I decided to create custom sidebars that mimicked their marketing strategy. Whenever someone lands on an article about angels, for example, the sidebar only shows other posts within the angels' category. This turned out to be the game changer that led to

Chapter 3: Your Schedule Is Killing Your Book Sales

a lower bounce rate and a higher subscription rate.

Change can be difficult for some people, so I made most of these changes over the period of a year in order to let my readers get use to them. The other reason it took that long was because I implemented ideas as they came to me and I had to look for the right plugins when they did. Unfortunately, not every blogger is so forthcoming with their closely guarded secrets.

If you run a Wordpress based blog, I strongly suggest adding the "Custom Sidebars" plugin, along with the "Extended Recent Posts" plugin. You'll have to set up a sidebar for each category if you want to mimic the strategies of YouTube and Amazon, but it is well worth the time it take to implement.

The 80/20 Rule of Marketing

If you're wondering what the 80/20 of marketing is, don't worry, you're in good company. The normal

80/20 rule says something to the affect of 20% of the people control 80% of the money.

When it comes to marketing, it means something a lot different. This is where I mess with your current schedule that you probably worked long and hard to make. 80% of your time should be spent marketing existing content, and 20% of your time should be spent creating new content. This is something that I learned from Derek Halpern of SocialTriggers.com.

This rule is the reason that you need to have your website up, running, and ready for visitors before you start marketing your material.

This rule has the potential to help breathe life into your old posts and projects, as well as your new ones. The main goal is to get the word out. Creating new content doesn't make much of a difference if nobody is reading your content to begin with.

A good place to start is by figuring out how much time you have to dedicate to your craft each day, and dividing it by ten. Then you need to figure out

Chapter 3: Your Schedule Is Killing Your Book Sales

which content you want to focus your time on, and I'll cover that in the following section.

Put Your Best Pen Forward

When you first start writing articles on your website, there are probably very few people reading them. Some of your articles might be very good, so what do you do? You can either let them die in your blogging graveyard or you spend your time giving them new life through marketing.

Just because an article is old to you, doesn't mean it's old to other people that haven't seen it. This brings us to the subject of creating "evergreen content". That phrase refers to content that is always relevant (how to sweep a floor) and not time sensitive (book fair this weekend).

Evergreen content is the content that you want to focus on promoting, even if it has been months or years since you wrote it. Time sensitive content needs to take priority when there is a deadline. After the deadline passes, get back to promoting your evergreen content.

Just because evergreen is always good, doesn't mean that is the only content that you should focus on. Current events in the news are another good way to bring traffic to your site, especially if you get an early jump on it. Just make sure that it is directly related to your niche.

Bending Social Media To Your Will

The awesome part about social media is how fast you can spread the word about absolutely anything. While you should definitely share your content with your family and friends, there is a much easier way to get new people to your blog, unless you're in the niche that teaches people how to make money online. Teaching people how to make money online is one of the hardest niches to break into because so many people want to do it, and there is a lot of money to be had. The competition is brutal.

Chapter 3: Your Schedule Is Killing Your Book Sales

Joining groups on Facebook and Linked In gives you the opportunity to post links to your articles that thousands of people will potentially see. Just make sure that the articles you post are relevant to the group's purpose. Posting irrelevant articles could get you banned.

What I've learned from promoting my ministry website and my business website is that almost everyone in the business group wants to promote their own project, so there is very little response. Like I said, the make money online niche is really cutthroat.

When you join groups based on a topic that people are really there to learn about, the response is vastly higher. Personally, I get about 200-300 visits from Facebook per day when I post my ministry articles in Christian groups. When I post my business articles in business and marketing groups, I may get 20-30 visitors on a good day.

A good strategy to employ is to find groups focused on your niche and promote your very best evergreen content. However, you don't want to spam the group, so only post links to your own content once per day, and always find at least two posts within the group, other than your own, to comment on.

This shows that you are there to participate and not there solely for the purpose of self promotion. It's also important that you don't post any "buy my stuff" type links. Nobody will buy your stuff and you'll probably get banned in the process.

"Many of life's failures are people who did not realize how close they were to success when they gave up." – Thomas Edison

Chapter 4: Any Niche Is Yours For The Taking

As we enter the last leg of our journey together, I want to let you know that any niche is yours for the taking. In my opinion, the strategies presented in this chapter are the most powerful weapon that you can have in your marketing arsenal.

The previous three chapters all focused on getting your content in front of fans in your niche. This chapter focuses on getting you recognized as an expert in your field by other experts in your field. Being recognized as an expert will also help you get your content in front of more people, but there are far bigger benefits to be had.

Just Take The Credibility You Want

There is a very closely guarded secret among marketers, and I stumbled upon it quite by accident before I ever read anything about it in a book or online. It is called "borrowed credibility". It is the reason that Oprah, Bill O'Reilly, Barbara Walters, and Howard Stern are the mega superstars that they are today.

What do these three have in common? Before they were famous themselves, they interviewed famous people. Once they got their foot in the door, they continued to interview more famous people. The more interviews they did, the more fame and credibility started to rub off on them until they became famous themselves.

Stop here and think about it for a moment. Besides The Color Purple, what was Oprah famous for before she started interviewing celebrities on her show? What was Howard Stern, Barbara Walters, and Bill O'Reilly famous for? Before Paris Hilton was famous for her leaked home video, perfume, reality shows, etc., she was famous simply because her last name was Hilton.

This is something that my friend and I stumbled upon when we started The Omega Hour. The very first interview we did was with Guy Malone, who is well known in the UFO and Christian community. It was this interview that convinced L.A. Marzulli, a bestselling Christian author, to take a chance and do the interview as well. After the ball started rolling,

Chapter 4: Any Niche Is Yours For The Taking

eventually Grant Jeffrey (bestselling Christian author), Chuck Missler (bestselling Christian author), Patrick Heron (bestselling Christian author), and Irvin Baxter (Christian TV host) appeared on the podcast. Even if you don't recognize the names, those within the Christian community usually do.

Over time, some of their credibility and fame started to transfer over to me, and I went from contacting people for interviews to people contacting me for interviews. You can take the same path to gaining notoriety in your niche as well.

Setting up a podcast is simple. I personally recommend BlogTalkRadio (Appendix B). It's free if your podcast lasts for 30 minutes or less, and all of your shows are automatically recorded and archived for you. If you want to create a longer show, there are different premium plans available to fit your needs.

The strategy here is to figure out which "big fish" in your niche that you want eventually have on your show. Once you figure that out, find out who their friends are in the field. Then find the friends of those friends, and so on. What you want to do is find the least famous one and ask to interview them.

Fame doesn't matter much among actual friends, but the less famous the person is, the more likely they are to jump at the chance to be interviewed, even if you don't already have a huge following. Once you've interviewed six or seven different people, it's time to reel in the "big fish".

After you get your first big name interview within your niche, make sure you drop the name when trying to book interviews with other important people in your niche. The more big names you can drop, the easier it'll be for you to get more big names, and so on. If your show is interesting, you will see your listener numbers increase with each show.

The reason this works so well is because celebrities are trusted by their fans. When they announce that they will be live on your show, their fans will tune in and some of them will like you. Those new fans will stick around to hear future shows. Every time you

Chapter 4: Any Niche Is Yours For The Taking

repeat this process, you gain new fans from another person's fan base.

Celebrities know about this concept, and that's why they are very careful about whom they associate with. It's also why celebrities date other celebrities, or hang out with other celebrities. Brangelina is more famous than both Brad Pitt and Angelina Jolie were on their own.

I'll give you another huge example of borrowed credibility. Shar Jackson and Brittney Spears both had kids by Kevin Federline (K-Fed). He was pretty much an unknown backup dancer and now he is regularly on TMZ and even released a rap album. How many examples can you think of? It definitely works.

The Omnipresent Author

The following concept is one that I learned from Pat Flynn of SmartPassiveIncome.com. He talks about being everywhere. When it comes to marketing on the internet, it's definitely possible to be a lot of places at once.

As your content starts to accumulate, you want to make sure that it is posted on as many of the major websites as possible. I suggest that you set up accounts on the following websites for starters, if you don't already have them:

1. Facebook
2. Twitter
3. YouTube
4. Linked In
5. Google+
6. Reddit
7. Tumblr
8. Before Its News

As you become more familiar with your niche, you'll also learn what other websites people in your niche like to frequent. While you are in the learning phase, the above eight websites should get a little bit of traffic flowing to your blog.

The next major step is getting your content syndicated. This isn't an easy task, so you should work on

Chapter 4: Any Niche Is Yours For The Taking

this throughout your writing career. There are generally two ways to go about this:

1. Professional Syndication
2. Self Syndication

Professional syndication is when a newspaper, magazine, or website picks up your column and spreads it to bunch of other newspapers, magazines, and websites. If you can pull this off, it could potentially give you exposure to thousands, and maybe even millions of people every week.

Self syndication works the same way, but you have to do it yourself. The one drawback that you have is that if you don't have permission to send your content to editors, it could be viewed as spam. Make sure you send an email and get their permission before submitting articles for consideration.

Getting your content syndicated can result in massive amounts of traffic, subscribers, and sales. It also helps further establish you as an expert in your niche. Once you get your website up and running, start contacting newspapers, magazines, and websites in your niche.

The last piece of information I want to give you is to apply to be a Guide on About.com. Not only do Guides earn a steady monthly income, they get thousands of visitors per day to their content. Be aware that there are lots of people competing for limited positions, so make sure you submit your best content for consideration.

Bestsellers Do It Better

And now ladies and gentlemen, I'm going to perform one of the greatest magic tricks on earth. I'm going to make all of your marketing inhibitions and apprehensions disappear.

Let's start at the beginning. What was it about this book that caught your attention? Was it the wording? The color? The size? The quote by Colin Powel on the back?

Chapter 4: Any Niche Is Yours For The Taking

Everything that attracted you to pick up the book and take a look at it was carefully crafted and thought out. Did you read the description on the back? What did you notice about it? I'm going to come back to these questions in a moment when I tell you about building an inner circle.

While I wouldn't call this book a marketing masterpiece, it is an example of more principles than what I've taught you so far. Now I'm going to reveal those other principles to you:

The Hook: You may have noticed that throughout this book, I would start to tell you something, then I'd tell you that I'd come back to it at a later point. That is a technique that is used to grab your reader's interest and keep them around until you come back to that point.

The key is to dangle a very interesting piece of information in front of them that they want to know, and then snatch it back with the promise to reward them with it if they stick around. This same strategy can be used in videos, audio, and in your writing. As you watch TV, YouTube videos, read magazines, etc., pay attention to how many times this strategy is used.

When used correctly, the hook pulls readers into the rest of your content and forces them to listen to what you have to say. As you get use to using this technique, you can use multiple hooks to achieve the maximum results.

Influence: In Chapter 2, I taught you about tapping your inner influence. Did you notice how often that I used mine on you? The reason you did the various things that I told you to do throughout this book was because I had your undivided attention.

You were seeking information from me, which put me in a position of power to influence your actions, even if was something small likes getting you to stop and think or having you go back and read something again. If you had any doubts about using your influence to move people to a desired result, lose them now.

Chapter 4: Any Niche Is Yours For The Taking

The Illusion of Choice – Giving someone the illusion of choice often gets them to choose the action that you desire them to take. There are various ways to create this illusion, but it works like this: you make your pitch, tell them the positives and the negatives, then end with:

- It's up to you.
- It's your choice.
- The decision is yours.
- You decide.

These are just examples, but once you find your voice, you'll know exactly what wording to use most effectively with your fans. Most people in general won't choose the negative option.

Urgency – This can be used in combination with the illusion of choice. Imagine this for a moment: you attend a conference with 100 people. At the end, the speaker gives you the opportunity to sign up for a free coaching class, but there are only 60 seats available. Who wants to be left out? Nobody wants to be left out. That list is guaranteed to fill up because it doesn't give people time to sit around and think about it. They know that there are 99 other people ready to take one of those 60 seats available.

Sell Yourself – When you looked on the back of the book, did I try to convince you to buy the book or did I convince you to buy into me as a professional? Feel free to look again if you don't remember.

The reason I started off telling you my credentials is because people invest in people first and in the product last. I know this from personal experience with my book, As The Days of Noah Were.

There are lots of people looking for the information that I provide in the book, but people that don't like me don't buy the book. People that like me buy the book. I've actually received emails from people that already owned the book, didn't like something I had to say on my Facebook page or blog, email me and tell me that they wish they hadn't bought the book.

It wasn't because of the books content, but because they bought into me. Keep that in mind as you pro-

Chapter 4: Any Niche Is Yours For The Taking

gress through your writing career, but also keep in mind that you can't please everyone all of the time. Some people just won't like you no matter what you do.

Build Your Inner Circle - One major key to the success I've had in writing is my inner circle. It consists of 6 people. There are 4 family members and 2 friends of the family. The reason they make up my inner circle is because they are brutally honest. The cover of this book is an example of their input.

The original prototypes were a green cover and a black cover. The vote was split down the middle, but it was my brother that didn't like either, so because of him I changed it to a light blue. My friend Taneka suggested that I change some of the wording on the cover and get the opinion of two additional people. My mom suggested that I change the red outline around the words to black. We all then agreed that the green cover should be tossed.

Once that was done, we voted between the black cover with the words outlined in red and the light blue cover with the words outlined in black. The vote was split 4 to 4, with me liking both. Taneka mentioned that a darker blue might work, so I changed it to a darker blue, and we voted again. This time the vote came out 8 to 1 in favor of the cover you see now.

This was all coordinated via text messages, with the exception of my wife and brother, who were here with me. Having an honest inner circle is key, if you want to be successful; no matter what it is you choose to do.

In closing, I want to encourage you to take action. That is the very first step on your journey to success, and it is also where most people fail. They plan and plan, but never take action. Don't put this off for weeks, months, or even years. Now is the time to do it. If you fail, get up, dust yourself off, and try it again.

I'm just a regular guy that decided to write for a living. I started with very little knowledge about effective marketing; I had no agent, and no publishing

Chapter 4: Any Niche Is Yours For The Taking

deal. My very first book failed, and I was ready to give up. The reason everything worked out for me was because I learned from my failure, got up, and pushed myself harder to succeed. I fully believe that you are capable of doing it too, and so I leave you with the following quote:

"Most great people have attained their greatest success just one step beyond their greatest failure." – Napoleon Hill

Thank You For Reading

Thank you for taking the time to read this book. I sincerely hope that it adds value to your writing career and that you use the strategies contained within the pages to take your book to the next level.

This book is just the first of several books in a series that focus on the topic of professional writing. If you would like to be notified when new books are released, please consider joining my mailing list. I've made it as convenient as possible to do so.

You can use your phone to scan the QR code at the bottom or you can go to the Virtual Business Training Network website at:

www.virtualbusinesstrainingnetwork.com

Interested In A More Personal Solution?

I have over 17 years of web development experience, and over 5 years of experience as an independent author. If you've run into a problem that this book can't help you solve or if you just want to take your writing career to the next level, I am available for coaching to help get you to where you want to be.

Coaching sessions last for two hours and during that time, you will have my undivided attention. In the past, I have charged as much as $500.00 per session, but if you mention this book, you will receive a special rate of $297.00 for two hours. That's a 41% savings!

However, there is one small catch. I limit myself to only one client per day, Monday through Friday, and I don't do any coaching on holidays or weekends. If you would like to book a coaching session with me, please use the following email to send me a message:

coaching@virtualbusinesstrainingnetwork.com

Appendix A

This marketing checklist should help get you off to a good start. You may need to modify it slightly to fit your current situation, so don't be afraid to do so if you have to.

- [ ] **Build Buzz Before Your Book Release**
    - Mention On The Radio
    - Write Articles
    - Start A Podcast
    - Post On Facebook
    - Post On Twitter
    - Post On Liked In
    - Post On Google+

- [ ] **Things To Put Inside Your Book**
    - Mailing List Page
    - Website Promo Page
    - Previous Books Page
    - Upcoming Books Page
    - Services Page
    - QR Codes

- [ ] **Before You Release Your Book**
    - Setup JV Partners
    - Setup Sales Page
    - Setup Landing Page

- [ ] **The Day of The Release**
    - Contact JV Partners
    - Notify Your Mailing List
    - Post To Social Networks

- [ ] **After The Release**
    - Write Articles About Subjects In Your Book
    - Link To Your Book Within Your Articles
    - Share Your Articles On Social Networks
    - Book Radio Interviews

Appendix B

This page contains all of the resources mentioned throughout this book. To make it more convenient for you, they are listed in alphabetical order.

Amazon Associates
https://affiliate-program.amazon.com

Aweber
http://www.aweber.com/?380976

BlogTalkRadio
http://www.blogtalkradio.com

Clickbank
http://www.clickbank.com/

QR Code Generator
http://www.qrstuff.com/

Toasmasters International
http://www.toastmasters.org

Wordpress
http://www.wordpress.org

Wordpress Plugins
http://www.wordpress.org

- Custom Sidebars
- Digg Digg
- Extended Recent Posts
- Thumbnail For Excerpts
- wp-polls

www.ingramcontent.com/pod-product-compliance
Lightning Source LLC
Chambersburg PA
CBHW071802200526
45167CB00017B/995